Munch, Munch, Munch!

Music and lyrics by Norma L. Gentner

Illustrations by Joe Veno

The caterpillars munch, munch, munch leaves for breakfast, leaves for lunch.

You ask me why
they do this?

To become
such beautiful things.

5

**The caterpillars
hide, hide, hide
in special shells
they'll grow inside.**

You ask me why
they do this?

To become
such beautiful things.

Then the pupae
sleep, sleep, sleep.
Each grows four wings
and six new feet.

You ask me why
they do this?

To become
such beautiful things.

Sleep, sleep, sleep, sleep, sleep, sleep, sleep, sleep, sleep!

13

The day has finally come, come, come, and to the twigs you'll run, run, run.

**You'll see
the caterpillars that...
became the beautiful things!**